SCOTTISH *life*

The Press and Journal

First published by

**Aberdeen Journals Limited, Lang Stracht,
Mastrick, Aberdeen AB15 6DF**

Acknowledgements

Contributions to the Scottish Life feature were made by Jayne Anderson, Christel Aspegren, Steve Bain, Raymond Besant, Bob Bruce, Ian Dawson, Stewart Fairlie, Bruce Irvine, Sandy McCook, David Murray, David Pattinson, Rory Raitt, Colin Rennie, Victoria Stewart and Ian Young.

ISBN 1 901300 05 6

Printed by Polestar AUP Aberdeen Limited

FOREWORD

The brief of members of the Press and Journal's photographic department was simple: go out and capture the essence of our territory. Take whatever you fancy and provide a daily picture for the paper's Opinion page.

They responded magnificently, bringing back a wide array of inspired work, including landscapes, people at work, subtle social comment and the occasional amusing item. The enthusiasm generated by the feature encouraged other members of staff to contribute, and now readers are sending in their entries.

On the threshold of the new Millennium, we decided to package the best staff pictures as a snapshot of the faces and places of North and North-east Scotland.

We hope it will provide hours of enjoyment, both for those who live in these parts and those who know it but who are now in other parts of the world.

Winter sunshine spills into St Magnus Cathedral, Kirkwall

Starlings take flight from their roosts under Union Bridge, Aberdeen

A view from the top of Bieldside, looking towards Deeside

Driftwood at Spey Bay

Looking over Cullen's Old Seatown towards the railway viaduct

Winter sunshine at Denman Park, Westhill, Aberdeen

The afternoon sun strikes Dunnottar Castle, near Stonehaven

Fish-filleter Sheena Fairlie at work at Abacus, Mintlaw

Winter sunset at Bennachie

Aboyne Loch glistens in the winter sun

Sunlight burns through the clouds on the East Coast at Crawton

Lochnagar from Loch Muick

A frosty path leads to Restenneth Priory, near Forfar

Slater Charlie Nicol repairs damage on a roof in the West End of Aberdeen

Charlie Morrison from Mason Lodge, Skene, with his 1960 Massey Ferguson 65 tractor.
He is competing in the Grampian Super Match at Knockiemill, near Turriff

A climber scaling the wall of Black Spout Gully, Lochnagar

Kelp farming at Warbeth, Orkney

The sands of Forvie nature reserve, near Newburgh, Aberdeenshire

Digger Hector Grigor takes time out for a photograph while working on the water main at Dunecht

Slains Castle near Cruden Bay

Statue at Aberdeen Art Gallery

The Falls of Dochart, Killin

Rhynie War Memorial and church

Ski-ing at the Lecht

Stan Bruce from Moss-side Farm, Leithall

Sandy Moir, stillman at Ardmore Distillery, Kennethmont, checks the spirit safe.

David McKessick, tree peeler with A. Gordon and Company, Sawmill, Bridgend, near New Pitsligo

The 16th Century Corgarff Castle against the February sky.

Tarlair swimming pool at Macduff

The winter sun shines down on Portmahomack harbour

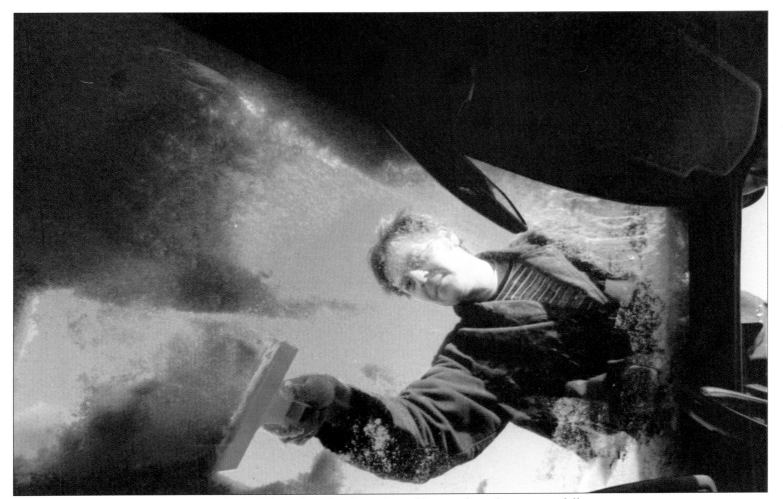

Richard Buglass, from Sauchen, cleans his car after a heavy snow fall

Pamela Latter and Margaret Hayes, on holiday from Cumbria, stroll near the river Dee at Ballater Golf Club

The coastline leading to Lerwick

Red deer in snow near Skene

A black-headed gull in winter plumage on an icy Duthie Park pond in Aberdeen

Pigs at Peattie Farm, Inverbie

A burn meanders through the snow-covered landscape near Dunecht, Aberdeenshire

The view from the bridge at Ballater, showing the Monaltrie Hotel

Winter view of Orphir moorland, overlooking Scapa Flow, Orkney

Old Midmar Kirk

Coalman Davie Slater prepares for his round

The little Spey at Kingston

Stormy weather near Fraserburgh

Aberdeen railway station

Ross Reid presides over his new greengrocer shop in George Street, Aberdeen

A robin enjoys a rest while looking for food on a winter morning

The harbour at Gourdon

Aberdeen beach seen through a porthole on a shelter

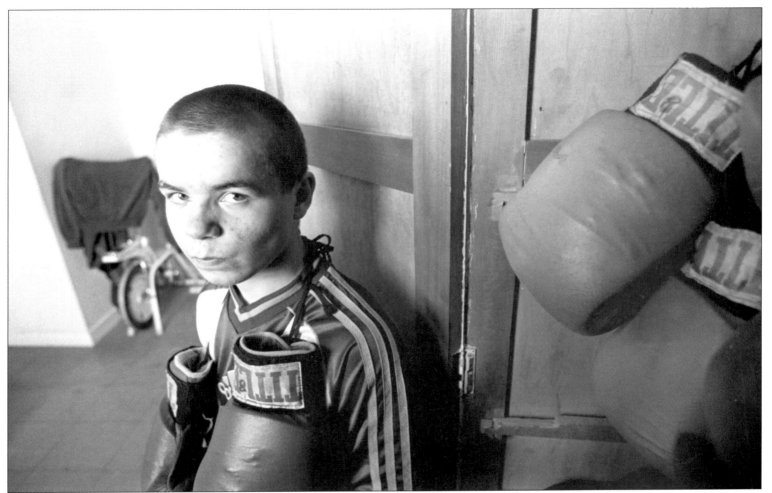

Young Aberdeen boxer Chris Cooper

George Scroggie waits in his cab ready for a load of rock salt from Cleveland, bound for the wintry roads of the North-east

Kite flying near Aberdeen beach

Jeffrey Cobb casts his line at Oldtown Fishery, near Newmachar

Sonja Flaws feeds the Shetland ponies at the Grutness and Laalsard Shetland Pony Stud, near Lerwick.

The seafarer monument at Montrose

King's College, Old Aberdeen

Drystane dykers Robert and Ester Morrison, of Inverurie, put their backs into it, constructing a wall near Banchory

A bright winter morning facing the cliffs of Beinn Dearg, near Ullapool

The head of Loch Duich and the peaks of Kintail from Ratagan

The Spey estuary at Kingston, looking east to Tugnet, with the Bin Hill of Cullen in the background

The coastline at Lerwick

The railway bridge at Montrose

The interior of St. Magnus Cathedral, Kirkwall

Clydesdale horses canter at Cullerlie Farm Park, Echt

The RGU boat prepares for the challenge against Aberdeen University

Waiting patiently in orderly fashion at Aberdeen harbour

Crew members carry out maintenance aboard the Highland Pride at Aberdeen harbour

Stone mason Raymond Watson working on Elgin Cathedral

The Black Cuillins of Skye, from Sligachan

Crouching down to enter Maeshowe in Orkney

The Calmac ferry Loch Striven takes passengers and cars to Raasay from Skye

The floodlit King's College Chapel, Old Aberdeen

Fisherman Jimmy Sinclair hauls in the day's catch on the creel boat Hildona, Stromness, Orkney

The sun shines on Glenfinnan monument

A sheep ignores the rules of the road near Cruden Bay, no ewe-turns please

James Smart rolls out the barrel at Ardmore Distillery, Kennethmont

The sun rising on a spring morning atop Dun Caan, on Raasay

The pond at Haddo House, Aberdeenshire

Kids enjoying the mild weather at Aberdeen beach on Easter Monday

A fishing boat passes the statue of the Madonna at the entrance to Knoydart

Farmers at Thainstone Mart, Aberdeenshire

Rehearsing at the Scottish Ballet in Glasgow

Feeding the birds at Duthie Park, Aberdeen

Walkers are dwarfed by the Rackwick cliffs on Hoy, Orkney

Rowing on the river Dee at Aberdeen

Parking meter attendant Peter Forbes checks the cars at the Castlegate car park in Aberdeen

Lobster creels at Johnshaven harbour

Geese walking in the flowers at Walker Dam, Aberdeen

An Lochan Uaine, or the Green Loch, between Glenmore and Abernethy, in Speyside

Looking towards Knoydart Estate in the spring sunshine

Stonehaven harbour at low tide

Simon Spalding playing outside the Maritime Musuem in Aberdeen's Shiprow

Sailing on the Loch of Skene, Aberdeenshire

Kayakers take a break after braving the chilly April waters off Aberdeen beach

The point where the river Deveron flows into the sea at Banff

An old plough lies rusting near Cammachmore

Jill Adron feeds her chickens at Maryfield farm near Banchory

A ghostly Marischal College, Aberdeen, shrouded in sea-haar

Highland cattle at Cults Farm, Strachan, near Banchory

Melvyn Morrice prepares for the reseeding of Victoria Park, Aberdeen

The bridge of Potarch, on Deeside, from the Strachan road

Tam Reid tends to the goats on his farm at Cullerie Park, near Echt

The harbour and village of Portsoy

A training exercise in the Minch for Stornoway Coastguards and a McBrayne ferry provides a tourist spectacle

View of Macduff from the anchor

Playing football in Northfield, Aberdeen

A misty day at John O'Groats

Shetland Golf Club on Dales Voe, near Lerwick

The shore front at Ullapool

Telford's bridge at Craigellachie

Hazel Brown and Margaret Donaldson enjoy a stroll near Drumtochty

A lone rower passes between the bridges on the lower Dee in Aberdeen

Drystane dyker Alan Smiles works near Lerwick

All is calm at the picturesque harbour at Whitehills

Water thunders down past the Brig of Feugh, near Banchory

An idyllic day with a loch reflecting the hills of Glencoe

Ally Oram shows his skateboarding skills on the half-pipe at Torry playing fields

Jock Edwards, from the Bigfoot Adventure Centre, Strathdon, takes a ducking

Storm clouds over the Mar Lodge Estate, Braemar

Children from the Quarryhill Primary School play at Aberdeen beach

The view over Aberdeen from St. Margaret's Church in the Gallowgate

View from the upper floor of the Bon Accord Centre in Aberdeen

Apples on a Fisherford window-sill

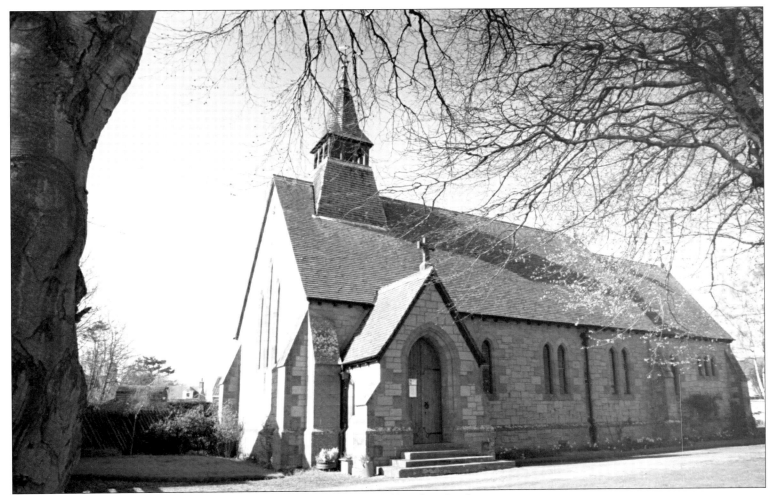

The Episcopal Church at Insch

Slains Castle at Cruden Bay

The sun goes down over Camusdarach beach, near Mallaig

Busy time for market-garden stallholders in the Green, Aberdeen

Marischal College, Aberdeen, from Broad Street

One of the residents of Butterfly and Insect World, Edinburgh

A tree lies where it fell at Linn of Dee during a storm

Two-year-old Reece Ewen takes in the wonder of the sea at Aberdeen beach, with his grandad Jim

Shielbridge, with the Five Sisters of Kintail in the background

Skye Bridge from Kyleakin

The river Dee as it runs past Mar Lodge Estate, Braemar

Bristow engineers wait for a helicopter to move off

Looking towards the Cuillins of Skye from Elgol

A disused boat on the shores of South Ronaldsay, Orkney

Toddlers Sarah Brown, Matthew Charlton and Eilidh Matheson enjoy a trip to the beach at Aberdeen

A horse rider enjoys the view towards the islands of Rum and Eigg

Glenfinnan Church

A view of Kitchener's memorial at the RSPB seabird reserve of Marwick Head, Orkney

A bonnie day at Whitehills harbour

Fishing on the Ness at Inverness

Natalie Finlay with her brother Christopher enjoy the sunshine, as they make sandcastles at Aberdeen Beach